My Early Surprise

A Bedtime Story for Preemies

Sharifa Brown

Softcover ISBN: 978-1-7361846-0-8
Hardcover ISBN: 978-1-7361846-1-5

Written By: Sharifa Brown
Illustrated By: Laurentiu Gabriel Dumitru
Publisher: Imagine Write Now, LLC

To the strongest soul I know– My Warrior– Malik Gerod Brown!
You are amazing and you will excel at whatever you decide
to do in life. I am forever amazed at your strength and
determination. I love you to the moon and back.
I am so excited to witness your journey of life.
I'm so proud to call you my son!

~Mommy

We prayed and prayed. Our dreams came true.
We were having a baby boy, and that baby was you!

At that moment, I loved you before I held you in my arms.
I made a vow to protect you and to keep you from harm.

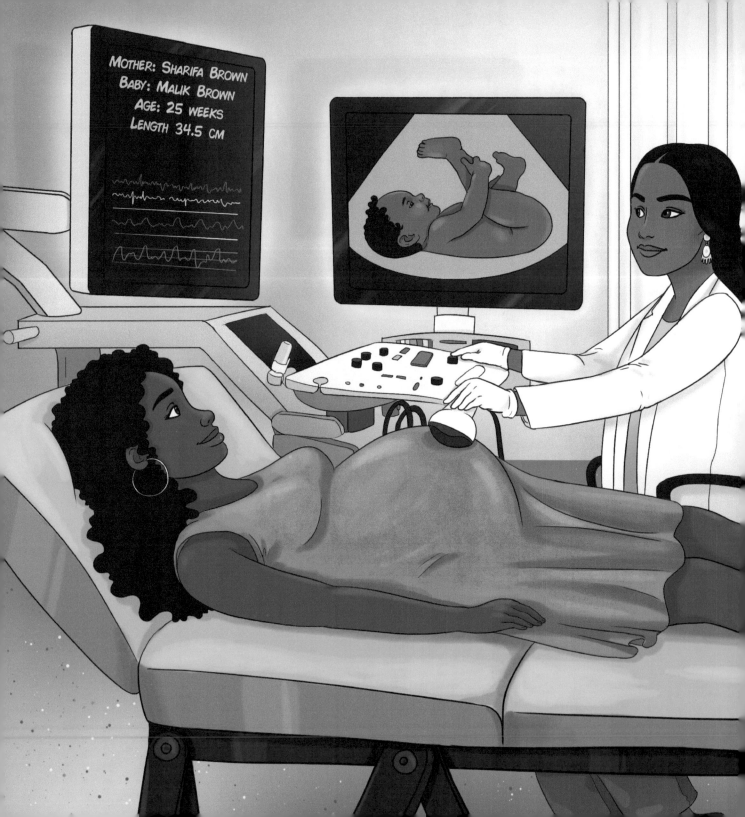

MOTHER: SHARIFA BROWN
BABY: MALIK BROWN
AGE: 25 WEEKS
LENGTH 34.5 CM

So as my tummy grew, so did my heart, more each day.
I loved to watch you on the monitor kick, wiggle, and play.

Then one day, I woke up in the middle of the night.
I was crying in pain and something wasn't right.

Thoughts rushed through my head, both hopeful and sad.
"Take me to the hospital!" I yelled at your dad.

The doctor came in and hung his head.
With a low, compassionate voice he said,
"I'm so sorry, ma'am. There isn't much we can do.
He is coming early, and we must prepare you."

"No, not now. We need more time,"
was the only thing I had on my mind.

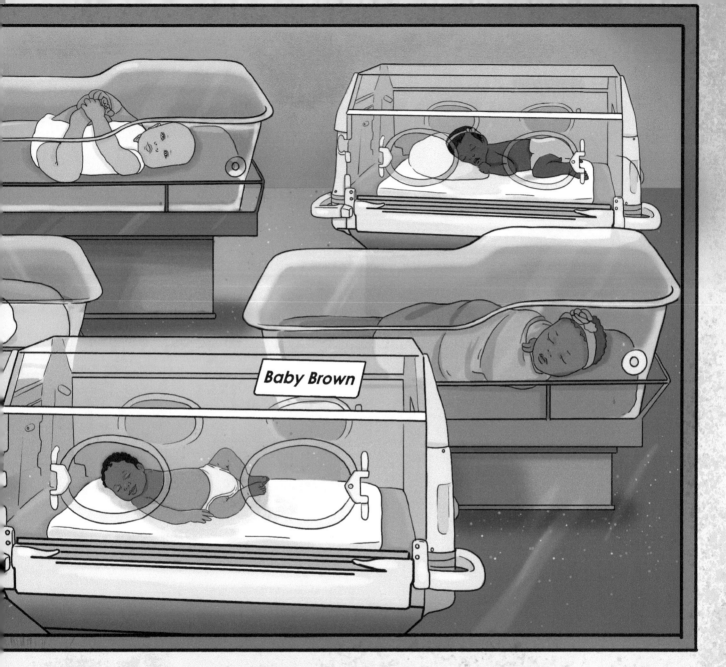

When you arrived you were so very small:
eyes closed shut with no crying at all.
Doctors were amazed: 2 pounds was your birth weight.
Healthy and strong, 3 months before due date!

Baby Brown

You were placed in a small box that was warm as well as clear.
I couldn't touch you, hold you, or let you know that I was near.
Your skin was smooth and sensitive to touch.
Oh, how I wanted to hold you so much!

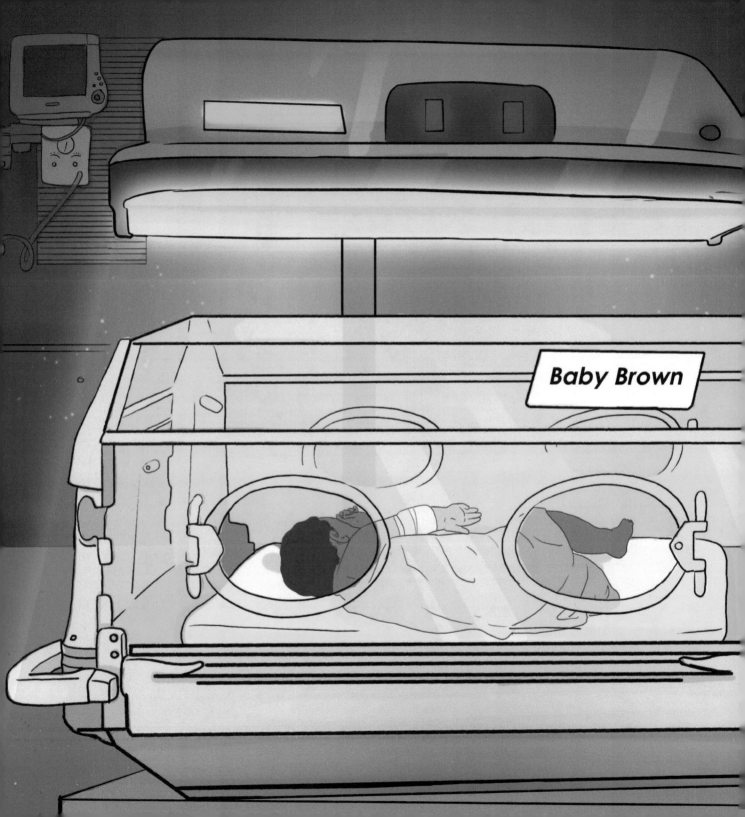

Your eyes were bandaged. You could not see.
Oh, please fight baby. Please fight for me!
Because you were so little, they bathed you with a light of blue
to get your body healthy and remove the yellow from you.

There were very smart people to make sure you would excel—
a preemie doctor, heart doctor, and a preemie nurse as well.

You needed special tubes to help you breathe and feed.
These well-built machines supplied your every need.

We would go to the hospital each and every day
to talk to the doctors and make sure you were okay.

Being away from you was such a hard thing to endure—
hearing good and bad news, never being sure.

Days turned to months, and I watched you grow:
accomplishing your milestones, "Go, Baby, Go!"
You maintained your temperature and took your first bottle.
You achieved all of this because YOU are unstoppable!

MALIK'S MILESTONES

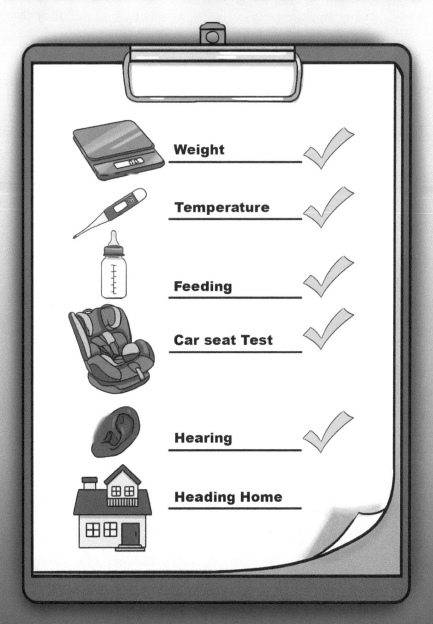

Weight ✓

Temperature ✓

Feeding ✓

Car seat Test ✓

Hearing ✓

Heading Home

You continued to strive; not once did you quit.
You showed me your will and amazing spirit.

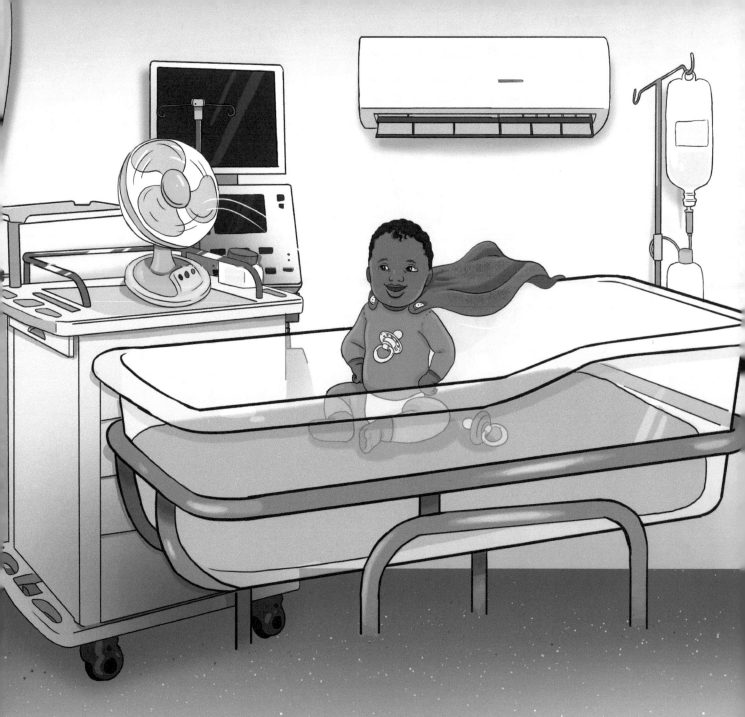

You showed me that you listened; you showed me your strength.
You amazed and shocked the doctors. You went to great lengths.

85 days have passed, and today is the day.
You are finally coming home with us to stay!

You are brave and will conquer whatever you do.
I thank God in heaven for giving me you!

So, whenever you feel down and get discouraged,
let me retell you this story of incredible courage.

But as for right now, lay your head down on me,
as I bask in the glory of being your Mommy.

CPSIA information can be obtained
at www.ICGtesting.com
Printed in the USA
BVHW020925270321
603524BV00002B/14